THE USBORNE SOCCER SCHOOL

TACTICS

Clive Gifford
Designed by Neil Francis

Illustrations by Bob Bond • Photographs by Chris Cole
Edited by Felicity Brooks • Managing designer: Stephen Wright
Consultant: John Shiels,
Bobby Charlton International Soccer Schools Ltd.

Thanks to Susan Robinson, Keely Flynn and Becky Flynn.
With special thanks to players Osman Afzal, Ben Dale, Mohammed Gulfam, Rachel Horner,
David Hughes, Moynul Islam, Michael Jones, Andrum Mahmood, Leanne Prince,
Daniel Savastano, Ciaran Simpson, John Tabas, Joe Vain,
and to their coaches, Bryn Cooper and Warren Gore.

Library photographs: Empics   Soccer boots courtesy of Reebok UK

DTP by John Russell

CONTENTS

WHAT ARE TACTICS?

In soccer, fitness and good ball skills are essential to success. But the way your team plays together is just as important. Tactics are the way a team is organized and how the players work with each other. Tactics can make all the difference between two closely-matched sides. When a less skilled side beats a better team, it can be luck, but is often more to do with team tactics.

PLAYING AS A TEAM

Any player, no matter how good, is still one out of eleven. You cannot just turn up and play your own game of soccer. You are part of a team. This is the single most important principle of soccer tactics.

The whole team must play according to the same plan to ensure its success. When learning about tactics, it is helpful to know the correct terms. The most commonly used terms are shown below.

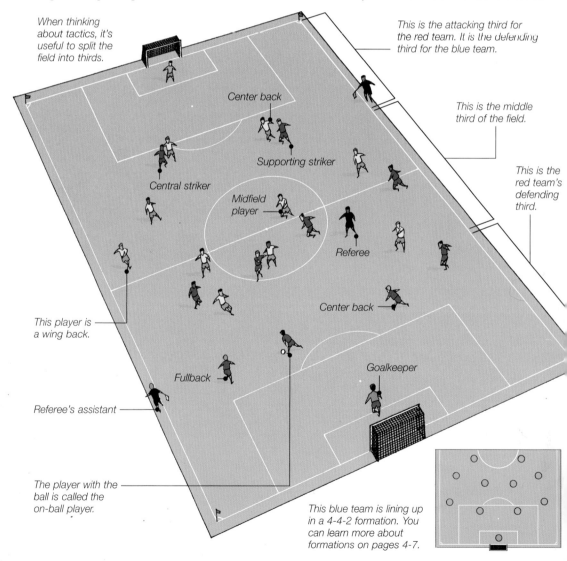

When thinking about tactics, it's useful to split the field into thirds.

This is the attacking third for the red team. It is the defending third for the blue team.

This is the middle third of the field.

This is the red team's defending third.

Center back

Supporting striker

Central striker

Midfield player

Referee

This player is a wing back.

Center back

Goalkeeper

Referee's assistant

Fullback

The player with the ball is called the on-ball player.

This blue team is lining up in a 4-4-2 formation. You can learn more about formations on pages 4-7.

2

FIELD MARKINGS AND MOVEMENT

Soccer fields may vary slightly in size, but they all have the same field markings.

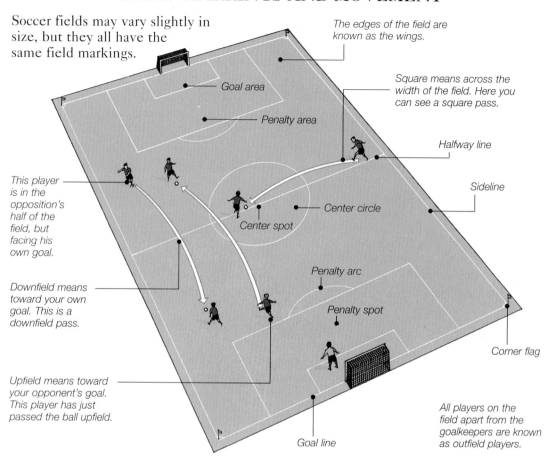

The edges of the field are known as the wings.

Square means across the width of the field. Here you can see a square pass.

Goal area

Penalty area

Halfway line

Sideline

This player is in the opposition's half of the field, but facing his own goal.

Center circle

Center spot

Downfield means toward your own goal. This is a downfield pass.

Penalty arc

Penalty spot

Corner flag

Upfield means toward your opponent's goal. This player has just passed the ball upfield.

Goal line

All players on the field apart from the goalkeepers are known as outfield players.

IN POSITION

Why don't teams with the best players win all of their games? Because it's a question of how these players are used. A team must use its players in the best way possible. For example, a right-footed player may find it very difficult to play on the left. The right-footed player in the picture has made a good run down the left wing. But he has to cut back to deliver a cross with his right foot, wasting time and losing his advantage.

See how as the winger cuts back, the defense can now cover him.

BE POSITIVE

Whatever tactics your team decides to use, you as an individual player must be positive about yourself and also your team-mates and the game officials. Never give up. Your team can be outplayed for almost the whole game, but still get to score a late goal and win. That's what makes soccer such an exciting game.

Paul Ince, playing here for England against Italy, still attacks with only moments left to play.

FORMATIONS

A formation is the basic shape of a soccer team. Most formations are described in numbers of outfield players from the defense forward. So 4-2-4, means four defenders, two midfield players and four attackers. To be successful, a team must have some shape so that players know where they should play and where their teammates will be. Successful formations balance attack and defense and make the best use of the players in a team.

FOUR-FOUR-TWO

The midfield area is an important area of the field. Teams often pack their midfield with players. 4-4-2 is a common, defense-minded formation. It relies on the forwards covering much ground.

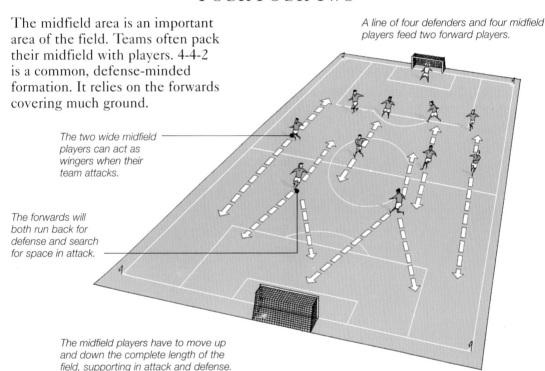

A line of four defenders and four midfield players feed two forward players.

The two wide midfield players can act as wingers when their team attacks.

The forwards will both run back for defense and search for space in attack.

The midfield players have to move up and down the complete length of the field, supporting in attack and defense.

FOUR-TWO-FOUR

In 4-2-4, two midfield players act as a link between the four men in attack and the four in defense. They must cover a huge amount of ground for the formation to work. Because of the huge strain put on the two midfield players, 4-2-4 is rarely played today.

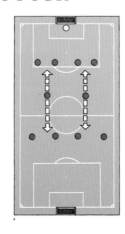

FOUR-THREE-THREE

4-2-4 is sometimes altered by dropping an attacking player back into the midfield to make a 4-3-3 formation. This yellow side has adopted a 4-3-3 formation with two central strikers and one winger. The winger may switch wings during the game, searching for openings.

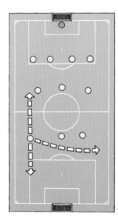

THREE-TWO-TWO-THREE

This system uses three center backs and two wing backs out wide. In defense, one of the center backs may be given the task of man-marking a particularly dangerous opposing forward. You can learn more about man-marking and defensive tactics on pages 10-11.

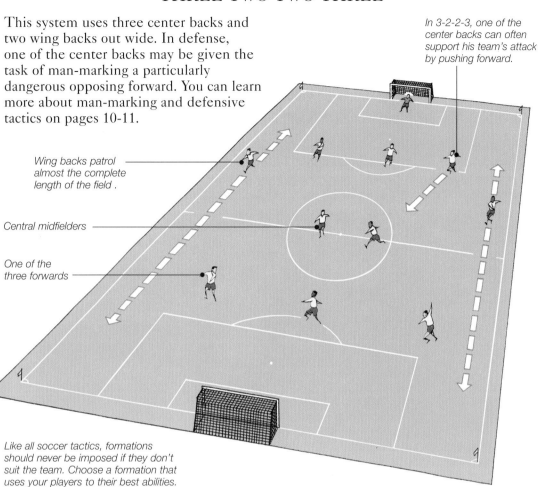

In 3-2-2-3, one of the center backs can often support his team's attack by pushing forward.

Wing backs patrol almost the complete length of the field .

Central midfielders

One of the three forwards

Like all soccer tactics, formations should never be imposed if they don't suit the team. Choose a formation that uses your players to their best abilities.

DEFLECTIONS AND LUCKY LONGSHOTS

No formations or tactics are foolproof. Sometimes, a bizarre event or piece of luck loses a team a game. You can't defend against a deflection off a player or an incredible long-range shot. Remember, just because your team has lost by a single goal does not necessarily mean that the formation and tactics you used were wrong.

No tactics can ever stop an overhead kick such as this spectacular effort by German striker, Jürgen Klinsmann.

FORMATIONS AND SYSTEMS

Systems are the way a group of players work within a complete team formation. In recent times, coaches and managers have worked on new formations and systems to give their sides an advantage.

CHRISTMAS TREE

This formation has four defenders, three midfield players, two attacking support players and a lone central striker, who is the farthest forward.

The formation provides good links between the midfield and the attackers. It relies on the two supporting attackers being flexible and working hard.

This supporting attacker must join the central striker at the right moment or roam wider and act as a winger.

This formation gets its name from the fir tree shape that the 4-3-2-1 arrangement makes.

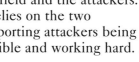

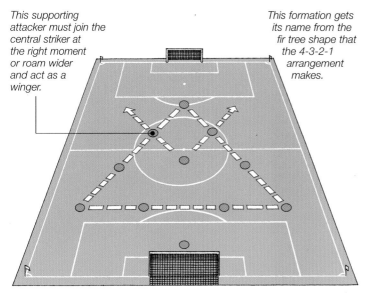

BEING FLEXIBLE

Some sides don't use a rigid formation. Instead, they use a flexible one where players in the best positions make forward runs or hang back to provide cover. A flexible system is hard to defend against, but requires excellent ability, fitness and communication between players.

National teams like Holland and Brazil, shown here, are famous for playing flexible formations in soccer.

VERSATILITY

Even if your team doesn't intend switching positions all the time, you should try to improve all of your soccer skills. Don't specialize in one position too soon. You can learn from playing in different positions, and it can be fun, too.

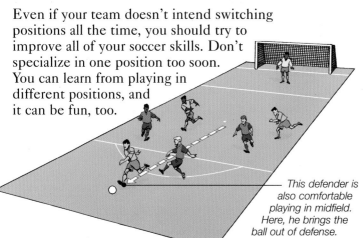

This defender is also comfortable playing in midfield. Here, he brings the ball out of defense.

Irish international, Roy Keane, plays in midfield and in defense, depending on what tactics his team is using.

SYSTEMS IN FORMATIONS

Within the framework of a formation, teams can play in different ways. For example, one team can play 4-4-2 defensively by pulling their forwards back behind the ball.

This team is playing an attacking 4-4-2. The midfield players push up to support the two strikers.

Within a formation, some players may play as part of an additional system. For example, the forwards and central midfielders in a team playing 4-2-4 may play the diamond system (see below).

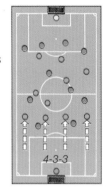

The defenders in a 4-3-3 formation can use the offsides trap (see page 13).

THE DIAMOND SYSTEM

The diamond system requires great discipline from the attacking players, but it is very hard to defend against. Ideally, the players will be able to play in all the different positions, rotating the diamond shape.

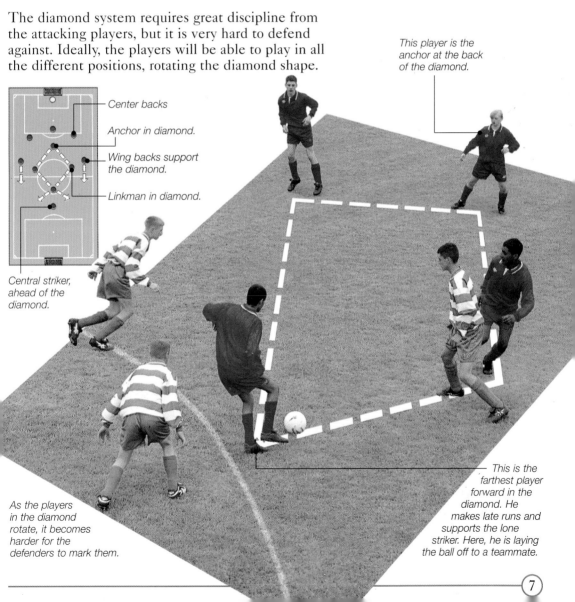

Center backs

Anchor in diamond.

Wing backs support the diamond.

Linkman in diamond.

Central striker, ahead of the diamond.

This player is the anchor at the back of the diamond.

As the players in the diamond rotate, it becomes harder for the defenders to mark them.

This is the farthest player forward in the diamond. He makes late runs and supports the lone striker. Here, he is laying the ball off to a teammate.

DEFENSIVE TACTICS

All successful teams, no matter how good their attack, always have a strong defense too. A good defense mixes individual skills and effective tactics. Defending is not just for defenders. The whole team is responsible for defense. This means, for example, that in man-to-man marking systems, midfield players mark opposing midfielders.

PRIORITIES IN DEFENSE

Defending is about stopping the other team from scoring goals. But as a defender you shouldn't just launch into a tackle.

When faced with an on-ball attacker, this is what you should try to do: **delay, deny, destroy** and **develop**.

This defender has closed up on the attacker. He's slowing the attacker down without giving him the space to go past.

This defender is forcing the attacker out wide. Notice that he isn't so close that the attacker can just burst past.

1. **Delay** the opponent to allow the rest of your defense to get into stronger positions. Get in his way to try to slow down the momentum of the attack.

2. **Deny** the opponent the position and space he wants. This means stopping him from turning to face the goal or shooting and forcing him away from danger areas.

Here, the defender has waited until he has cover before he commits himself to winning the ball cleanly.

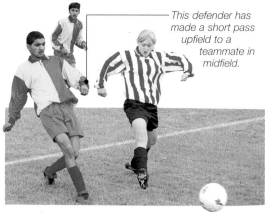

This defender has made a short pass upfield to a teammate in midfield.

3. **Destroy** the attack by challenging your opponent for the ball. You can do this either by tackling him directly or by intercepting a pass.

4. **Develop** play. Once you have the ball, you need to get it away from your goal and develop an attack for your team. You may be able to pass or continue a run yourself.

PROVIDING COVER AND SUPPORT

It's essential for defenders to communicate with and support their teammate who's facing the on-ball attacker. Defenders should try to provide direct cover in case the attacker gets past the on-ball defender.

This defender has stepped back toward goal. This is called 'sagging back' and it helps stop an attacker from making a penetrating run.

Direction of play

This is the on-ball defender.

This defender provides cover for the on-ball defender and keeps an eye on the winger moving down the line.

WORKING AS A TWO-MAN UNIT

With two defenders in position, you can do more than just delay an attacker. Once you have cover, you can think about a direct challenge, or two players can work together to squeeze the ball away from the attacker.

The on-ball defender can position himself slightly to one side of the attacker, forcing the attacker toward a second defender. Here, the second defender has 'sagged back', both to provide cover and watch the second attacker.

If the on-ball attacker passes the ball, the defenders can slide around to continue the same move on the new on-ball attacker. The two defenders must communicate with each other for the move to be successful.

This defender is providing cover, so that the on-ball defender can make his tackle.

The off-ball defender can move in and tackle the attacker in a move sometimes known as double-teaming. This move should be timed to surprise the attacker, giving the defenders a good chance of gaining the ball.

MARKING SYSTEMS

Defending as an individual is important, but so is the type of marking system you use. Your team has to decide whether to go for man-to-man, zonal or combination marking (see page 27).

MAN-TO-MAN MARKING

In man-to-man marking, your defenders and some or all of your midfield players, are each assigned an attacker to mark throughout the game. These players watch their attacker and stick close to him when the other team has the ball. Man-to-man marking works well in your defending third with spare players, such as your attackers, putting pressure on the opposing player with the ball. Each defender can be matched up against an opponent's specific skills. As the game progresses, you can identify any weaknesses of the player that you are marking.

Scottish international defender, Colin Hendry, is particularly good in the air. He usually man-marks the opposing side's most dangerous aerial attacker.

MARKING GAME

Play five-a-side for 20 minutes. You each mark a player when his team has the ball. When your team has it, the object is to get away from your marker.

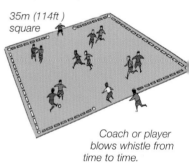

35m (114ft) square

Coach or player blows whistle from time to time.

Players should stop as soon as the whistle is blown. Each defender should be within touching distance of the player he is marking. If not, he should go in goal or take over the whistle from the player on the sideline.

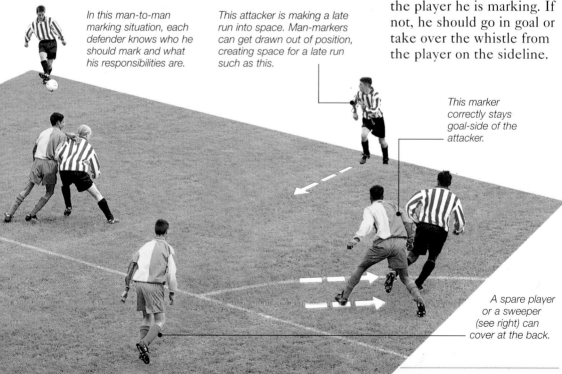

In this man-to-man marking situation, each defender knows who he should mark and what his responsibilities are.

This attacker is making a late run into space. Man-markers can get drawn out of position, creating space for a late run such as this.

This marker correctly stays goal-side of the attacker.

A spare player or a sweeper (see right) can cover at the back.

ZONAL MARKING

Zonal marking means you defend an area of the field. Each defender is assigned a zone which overlaps with neighboring defenders' zones. Unlike man-to-man marking where defenders can be dragged around the field, zonal marking helps keep the defense together in a compact shape.

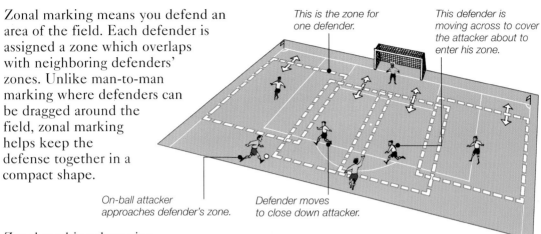

This is the zone for one defender.

This defender is moving across to cover the attacker about to enter his zone.

On-ball attacker approaches defender's zone.

Defender moves to close down attacker.

Zonal marking does give attackers more time and space. It requires good awareness of the area you're defending. Communication between defenders must be good, especially when handing over a moving attacker from one zone to another.

Although defenders must know where the ball is, they should not ball watch. Instead, they must be aware of the play as it develops and particularly, any attackers straying into their own zone or neighboring ones.

Zonal marking can create an overload in defense (more defenders than attackers) in areas near its goal. This makes it much harder for the attacking side to score. Both defenders and attackers seek to obtain overloads whenever possible.

This defender has no attacker in his zone. He provides cover for the on-ball defender and can join him in his zone to put more pressure on the attacker.

This defender decides whether to delay the attacker, force him one way or tackle him.

The defender farthest from the action should be in a good position to see how play develops.

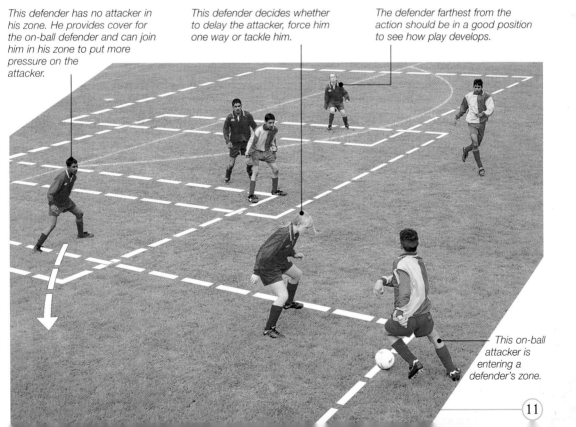

This on-ball attacker is entering a defender's zone.

ADVANCED DEFENSIVE TACTICS

There are various other defensive tactics your team can employ. Among the most common are using sweepers, offsides traps and the wall defense.

THE ROLE OF THE SWEEPER

The sweeper is so called because he usually plays behind the defense, sweeping up any loose balls or attacks that get past the main defense. A sweeper has to be very agile and good at 'reading' the game. Along with the goalkeeper, he should organize the defense, directing the other defenders and making sure they are in the correct place.

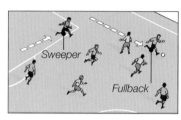

Sweepers provide cover when another defender has the ball. This sweeper has passed to his fullback, and is providing cover in case the fullback loses the ball.

Sweepers don't man-mark, but there are times when an unmarked attacker appears in the defense. This sweeper is picking up the unmarked attacker.

Another role of the sweeper is to cut out through balls. Here, this sweeper reacted early to intercept a potentially dangerous pass.

Sweepers can also start an attack. The sweeper above has taken the ball and is moving forward to link with midfield. Because sweepers are rarely marked, they can add surprise and variety to the attack.

The sweeper can now move upfield with the ball.

WALL DEFENSE

Mattheas Sammer, the German sweeper, covers for his teammates, mopping up any loose balls and quickly closing gaps.

The wall defense is when three or four defenders line up across the field with a defensive sweeper behind them. This is a very defensive measure used to restrict goal-scoring chances. Midfielders and even attackers fill much of the remaining space between their goal and the attacking team. With so many players behind the ball, it makes it hard for the team playing this defense to launch an attack. Teams using the wall defense rely on fast breaks by small numbers of fast-moving attackers to score.

PLAYING AN OFFSIDES TRAP

A player is offsides if, when the ball is played, he is in the other team's half and there are fewer than two defenders closer than him to the goal line. An offsides trap is where a defense pushes up in a line square to the field. By doing this quickly, the defense can catch opposing forwards offsides. It's a risky tactic, especially if the referee's assistants are not experienced. If your team intends to play the offsides trap, make sure every player knows how to do it.

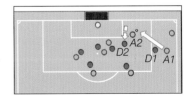

The red team are defending.

Here is an offsides trap played at a corner. A1 has received a short corner pass. The defense push up, keeping goal-side of the ball.

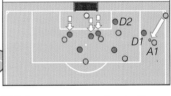

D1 is nearest to the ball. He closes down A1. D2 has moved from the goalpost to provide cover.

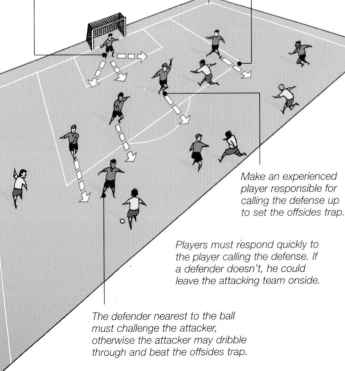

The goalkeeper should be prepared to cover his defense in the role of a sweeper if necessary.

Use field markers, such as the edge of the penalty box, to get your defensive line straight.

Make an experienced player responsible for calling the defense up to set the offsides trap.

Players must respond quickly to the player calling the defense. If a defender doesn't, he could leave the attacking team onside.

The defender nearest to the ball must challenge the attacker, otherwise the attacker may dribble through and beat the offsides trap.

D2 must be level with his defending teammates to catch the blue attackers offsides. He must move away from his goal before A2 receives the ball.

MIDFIELD AND DEPTH

As a game progresses, your team will find itself continually shifting between attack and defense. Midfield players are constantly involved in both these phases, so they must know all about the tactics for attacking and defending.

The midfield is where the ball is most often won and lost. Midfield players have to be strong tacklers, incredibly fit and read the game well. When their team is defending, they must get back goal-side of the ball as quickly as possible. In attack, midfield players should provide support to their attackers.

The red team's midfield use the ball to launch an attack.

ATTACKING WITH DEPTH

Midfield players can help stagger an attack, giving it depth up and down the field. Depth gives the on-ball attacker a safe pass behind him if he runs into trouble. There is nothing wrong with passing the ball back to keep possession until your team finds a good attacking opening.

The defenders are drawn to this attacker who plays the ball back.

This player runs into space looking for a pass.

The space was created by the attacker using depth.

By giving an attack depth, a team gives itself more options. This team has attacked with depth. They have created valuable space for a penetrating pass.

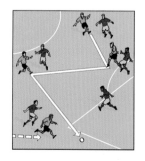

An attack without depth often breaks down. This team has attacked in a flat line. As a result, an attempted pass has been intercepted by the opposing defense.

CHANGING TACTICS

Top teams have coaches and managers who signal changes in tactics from the sideline or make changes at half-time. Top players are well coached and can slip into a new playing pattern easily. When you are losing badly, playing with less than a full team or suffering from injuries, a switch in tactics may be the answer. Otherwise, try to avoid unnecessary changes during a game.

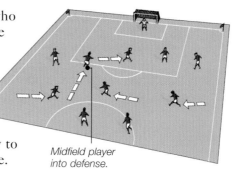

Midfield player into defense.

This team is changing from 4-4-2 to 5-3-2. They are adding an extra defender.

SUBSTITUTES

Substitutes aren't just for injuries, they can be used as a tactical tool as well. You can replace struggling players with fresh ones. These may have different skills which will create new problems for the opposing team. You can also protect a lead by replacing a striker with a more defensive player.

Even top stars such as Dutch winger, Marc Overmars, sometimes find themselves being substituted.

DOWN TO TEN MEN

If a player gets ejected, or injuries reduce your team to ten players, changes have to be made. Ten-man teams can make the mistake of becoming too defensive. This means that with no forward players, clearances just go straight back to the other team. Try to keep players forward if you can.

Wing back sent off.

With a player ejected, this team reorganizes from 3-2-2-3 to 4-3-2.

KEEP WINNING

Any team can score a lucky goal, but to get two or more ahead is not just luck. It usually means your team has a definite advantage over the other team. Don't relax just because you're winning. Keep trying to use that advantage the best you can.

These two players in yellow and green are defending hard even though their team is winning 3-0.

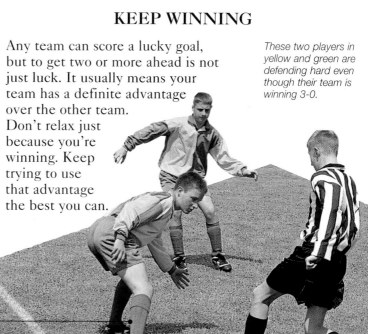

This defender is forcing the attacker to the right, where the second defender is placed.

POSSESSION

Much practice concentrates on gaining possession of the ball, but just as important is learning how to keep it. You need to practice with other players to learn this skill. Good awareness and passing is important, but you must have someone to pass the ball to safely. Teammates must support the player on the ball in order to keep possession.

KEEPING POSSESSION

Playing mini-games in small areas is a good way of learning to keep possession. In this 3 v 1 game, the team of three tries to keep possession of the ball for as long as possible. The game stops when they lose the ball or it leaves the box.

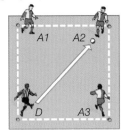

D has passed to A2. After A2 has touched the ball, D has started to close A2 down.

A1

A2

D

A3

A1 and A3 are in good supporting positions. A2 can see them and pass to them as D approaches.

The markers show an 8m (26ft) square.

TEMPO

Tempo means the pace of the game. The tempo of soccer in some leagues is very high. This means that the game moves fast and pressure is applied to the players in possession of the ball in all areas of the field.

Top club sides such as Barcelona play a more defensive formation and look to slow the game's tempo down when playing away from home.

The tempo of the game can also be slowed by getting players back behind the ball and keeping possession for long periods. Good teams can vary the tempo, slowing the game down when defending, and then attacking quickly when pushing forward. Great teams can control the tempo of the game effectively.

LONG BALL TACTICS

A long ball cuts out the midfield and lands in the attacking third of the field. Playing the long ball is risky. There's a chance your team may lose possession, but there's also the chance that you will gain a great attacking position. If your attacker gets the ball, teammates can run upfield to join and support him.

The long ball depends on accurate passing skills from defense. The long ball is aimed at an attacker who is strong in the air and must come to meet the ball. Even the best attackers only win and control some long balls.

This long ball is aimed at one of this team's two attackers.

This defender intercepts the long ball easily.

This attacker has not gone to meet the long ball.

This target attacker has waited for the long ball to reach him. But because a long ball takes time to arrive, defenders can anticipate the ball's flight and intercept it.

WORKING ON THE LONG BALL GAME

If you ever see your attacking third containing only one or two of your attackers with an equal number of defenders, consider playing the long ball.

Work on playing the long ball with the game shown in the picture to the right. Play 4 v 4 in the middle area of the field and 1 v 1 in both attacking end zones. Players in the 4 v 4 area can only pass into their end zone when they are inside their half of the field.

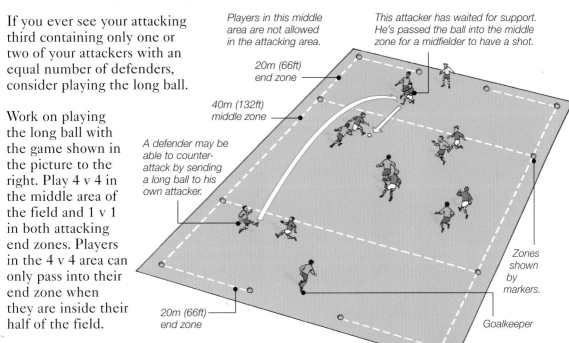

Players in this middle area are not allowed in the attacking area.

This attacker has waited for support. He's passed the ball into the middle zone for a midfielder to have a shot.

20m (66ft) end zone

40m (132ft) middle zone

A defender may be able to counter-attack by sending a long ball to his own attacker.

Zones shown by markers.

20m (66ft) end zone

Goalkeeper

ATTACKING TACTICS

To score goals you've got to create attacking chances. Your team must attempt to get the ball to teammates in clear goal-scoring positions.

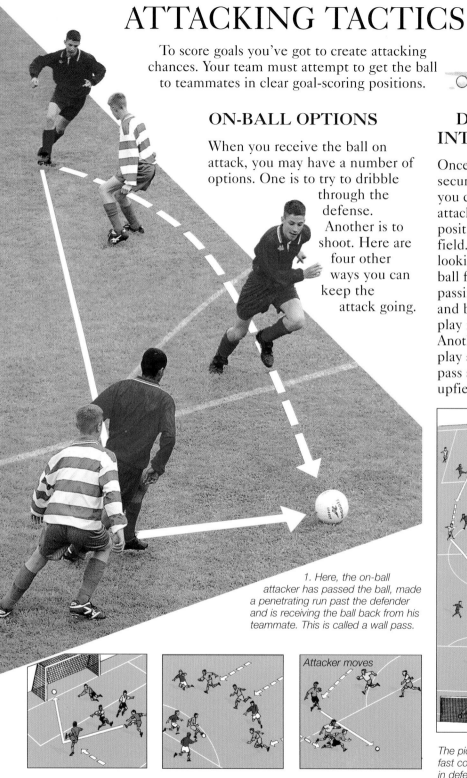

ON-BALL OPTIONS

When you receive the ball on attack, you may have a number of options. One is to try to dribble through the defense. Another is to shoot. Here are four other ways you can keep the attack going.

DEFENSE INTO ATTACK

Once your team has secure possession, you can launch an attack from any position on the field. You should be looking to move the ball forward by passing, running and building the play in midfield. Another option is to play an early long pass straight upfield.

1. Here, the on-ball attacker has passed the ball, made a penetrating run past the defender and is receiving the ball back from his teammate. This is called a wall pass.

2. The on-ball attacker could pass to a player in a better shooting position.

3. The attacker could hold possession and wait for support from teammates.

Attacker moves

4. He could move into a better position to shoot, or make an attacking pass.

The picture above shows a fast counter-move. Starting in defense, the ball is passed into midfield before a long direct pass is made to a forward player.

GOALIE'S DISTRIBUTION

The goalkeeper can start an attack in several ways. He can guarantee his team possession by passing or throwing the ball to one of his defenders. If he has intercepted a cross or through ball, he can also kick a long ball upfield quickly. Since the other team was moving forward on attack, a well-placed kick may find their defense out of position.

SUPPORT IN ATTACK

No attacker with the ball should ever be isolated. He should receive support from his teammates. There are four principles behind how a team can and should support the on-ball attacker. These are depth (see page 14), width, mobility and penetration (see page 20-21).

A player with the ball, but no support will most likely lose possession. In this picture, the player's teammates are working hard to provide him with a number of options.

Attackers making runs

GIVING AN ATTACK WIDTH

Using the full width of the field stretches a defense and creates more space for an attack. Defenders are either unable to mark players on the wings, or they move wide, leaving space in central areas. This space can be filled by other attackers.

You don't have to play wingers to use width in attack. Fullbacks or wing backs can come up and support, providing an extra option.

Ryan Giggs often drifts wide, away from the defense to receive the ball. He then uses his pace and skillful ball control to set up an attack.

This fullback is unmarked and is making an overlapping run on the outside.

MOBILITY AND PENETRATION

Mobility in soccer often means making runs to support the attack. Runs help the on-ball attacker by providing him with more options. Runs can also create more space for the on-ball attacker by drawing defenders away from him and to the player making the run.

MAKING DIAGONAL RUNS IN ATTACK

Defenders find it easiest playing against attackers who make moves straight up and down the field. These allow defenders to mark and cover. If you make diagonal runs, however, you can create confusion in the defense. Defenders are unsure whether to go with you or to mark the space. Defenders are most worried about the space between them and their goal. So, a move away from their goal can free you of your mark.

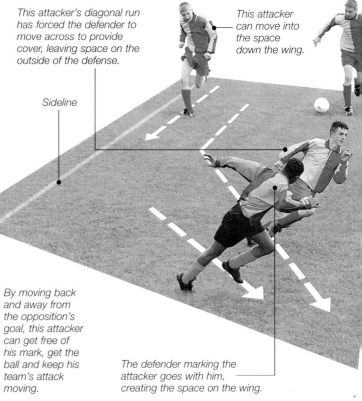

This attacker's diagonal run has forced the defender to move across to provide cover, leaving space on the outside of the defense.

This attacker can move into the space down the wing.

Sideline

The defender marking the attacker goes with him, creating the space on the wing.

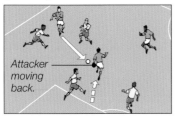

Attacker moving back.

By moving back and away from the opposition's goal, this attacker can get free of his mark, get the ball and keep his team's attack moving.

BLINDSIDE RUNS BEHIND A DEFENDER

Blindside running is when a run is made behind a defender. The attacker can see both the defender and the ball while he makes his run. The defender, on the other hand, can only watch the ball coming from one direction and the opposing player from another. This can make the defender indecisive which gives attackers an advantage.

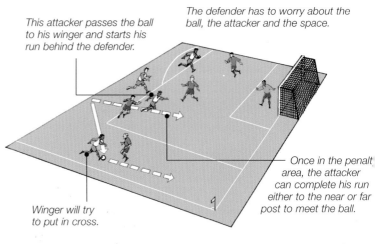

This attacker passes the ball to his winger and starts his run behind the defender.

The defender has to worry about the ball, the attacker and the space.

Winger will try to put in cross.

Once in the penalty area, the attacker can complete his run either to the near or far post to meet the ball.

PENETRATION

Penetration is getting into the attacking third of the field and behind the defense, while staying onside. Without penetration, attackers can only resort to long distance shots. To support the on-ball attacker, other players try to penetrate the opposition's defense. These players try to time their runs carefully to receive the ball in a shooting position or to act as decoys. Decoy runs help move defenders away from certain areas, creating space for other attackers. It is when players are trying to penetrate an opposition's defense that they are most likely to be called offsides.

See how this player has switched his run to the right, confusing his marker.

The on-ball attacker can dribble or pass into the space created by his teammates' runs.

The second penetrating attacker has cut to the left. He draws his defender with him, creating more space for the pass.

LAYING OFF THE BALL

The attacker farthest forward will try to penetrate the defense before he receives the ball. After controlling it, this player may pass the ball a short distance back or sideways to a supporting attacker, a move called 'laying off'. Laying off helps bring other players into the attack.

This player has controlled the ball before laying it off to a supporting teammate.

Once the ball is laid off, attackers should start runs. Defenders often watch the ball as it is laid off, giving attackers a split second to get free.

Lay off

Pass

You could work on laying off with a friend. One player delivers a long pass and moves forward to get the lay off. The other player controls the ball and lays it off. Repeat the move, switching the roles around.

SHOOTING TACTICS

Soccer is about scoring goals. Goals and nothing else win games. Some goals come from headers which require good, accurate crosses. Most goals, though, come from shots.

This player has more space and time to shoot.

SHOOT OR PASS?

Every player should work on his shooting. In modern soccer, especially now that the forwards are so heavily marked, goals are expected from other sources, including central defenders and fullbacks.

Don't be afraid to shoot. It only takes one well-hit shot to win a game. But, it's always worth checking to see if a teammate is in a better position to shoot than you are.

This attacker had time on the ball, but two defenders were blocking his shot at goal.

A quick square pass sets the far player up with a good shooting chance.

SHOOTING SIMULATION

Try to simulate shooting in game conditions by placing attackers and defenders between you and the goal. Don't just shoot from a standing position. In a real game, you are far more likely to be kicking a moving and bouncing ball. To simulate this, get someone to throw, pass or bounce the ball to you before you shoot.

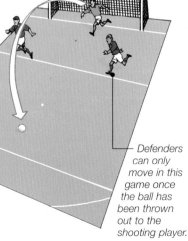

Defenders can only move in this game once the ball has been thrown out to the shooting player.

STAR SHOT

Midfield player David Beckham is in a good position as he shoots. He has his non-shooting foot beside the ball and his body over the ball.

FIVE AGAINST FIVE SHOOTING GAME

Much shooting practice consists of hitting shots past a lone goalkeeper. Unfortunately, shooting chances like these are rare. Usually, your shot will have to beat defenders as well as the goalie. The picture on your right shows a fun 5 v 5 mini game, but on an unusually-shaped field which is 35m (114ft) long.

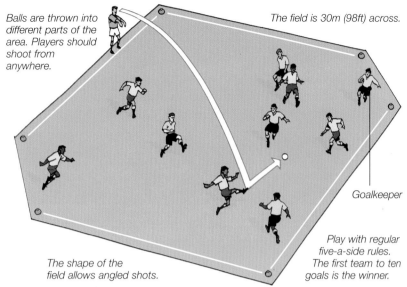

Balls are thrown into different parts of the area. Players should shoot from anywhere.

The field is 30m (98ft) across.

Goalkeeper

The shape of the field allows angled shots.

Play with regular five-a-side rules. The first team to ten goals is the winner.

SNAP SHOOTING GAME

Divide a goal into four imaginary boxes. Label them A, B, C and D. One player passes the ball and calls out a box name. The other player must turn and shoot immediately. Concentrate first on quick shots on the whole goal with few or no touches. Then work on hitting the correct box.

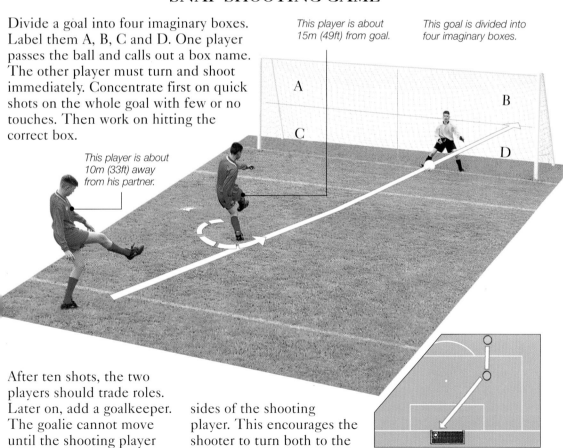

This player is about 15m (49ft) from goal.

This goal is divided into four imaginary boxes.

This player is about 10m (33ft) away from his partner.

After ten shots, the two players should trade roles. Later on, add a goalkeeper. The goalie cannot move until the shooting player touches the ball. The player should pass to both sides of the shooting player. This encourages the shooter to turn both to the left and right, not just to his favorite side.

Try standing to one side of the goal to work on more angled shots.

SET PLAY TACTICS IN ATTACK

Set plays are moves planned in practice by a team, usually from restarts such as free kicks, throw-ins and corners. Many goals are scored from set plays. They should be rehearsed frequently so that you and your teammates know exactly what you are doing.

FREE KICKS

Choose just a few free kick moves to work on. Don't make them too elaborate. You may end up confusing yourselves, not your opponent.

Ball passed to the right of the row of defenders.

WORKING ON CROSSES

Many goals come from quick, accurate crosses, both from corners and in open play. All players should practice crossing the ball. In the game below, you need at least three outfield players and a goalkeeper.

The attacker should come to meet the ball. He must get there first before the defender.

The crosser should vary the types of crosses he sends in. This cross is to the feet of the attacker.

This far post cross is met by the attacker who has moved back to get behind his marker.

This cross is into space in front of the attacker. It's a hard ball to defend and a bad tackle can mean a penalty.

After some time, add more pairs of attackers and defenders. This demands more accurate crosses and tighter defending.

If you're first to the ball, you have a better chance of getting a header or strike at goal. The defender has to think about both ball and player. If he just watches the ball, the attacker can fake and get clear of the defender.

BEATING AN OFFSIDES TRAP

An attacking team must be patient. Even the best offsides trap can break down and the attack can be given a clear run at goal.

Remember, a player is not offsides if he is level with the last outfield defender on the field. Here are some more helpful tips.

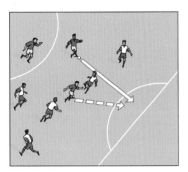

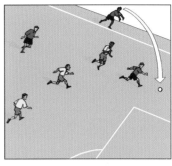

Time your run. This attacker has delayed his run long enough to stay onsides until the ball is eventually played.

Disguise your play. This attacker faked a pass, but instead, dribbled through the defense which pushed up for offsides.

Think quickly from a restart. You cannot be offsides if you receive the ball directly from a throw-in, goal kick or corner.

ATTACKING THROW-INS

Throw-ins can be a great attacking weapon. Long throws are as good as a cross, while quick throws can catch a team off guard. As with all restart situations, always be aware of the quick move. Here's a simple throw-in move down the line which involves drawing a defender to create space for a fullback to receive the ball.

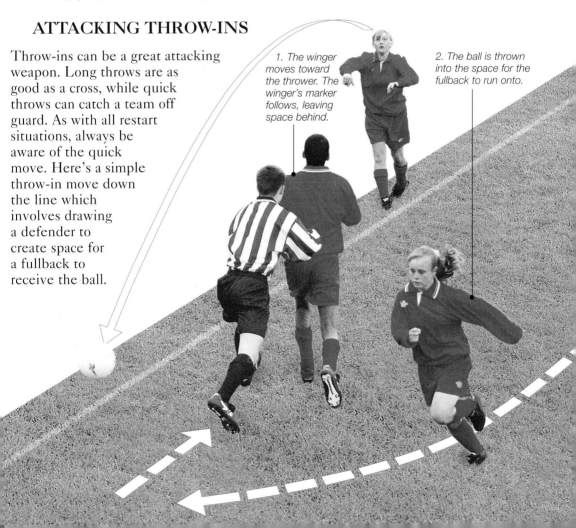

1. The winger moves toward the thrower. The winger's marker follows, leaving space behind.

2. The ball is thrown into the space for the fullback to run onto.

SET PLAY TACTICS IN DEFENSE

With so many goals scored from set plays, defenders must concentrate. Teams should quickly organize their defense as soon as a corner, free kick or throw-in is given.

DEFENDING AT CORNERS

For corners and free kicks within scoring range, defenders should listen to their goalkeeper as he organizes a free kick wall or positions defenders.

Goal-line defenders can block a shot if the goalie fails to clear or catch the corner.

This attacker has gotten behind his marker and is in a good attacking position. Always stay goal-side of your man when defending.

Defenders must cover both posts. These are common targets for corners.

Other defenders should be marking attackers who make runs into the penalty area as the corner is taken.

PASS-BACKS

If a defender deliberately passes the ball back to the goalie with any part of his body except his head, the goalie cannot use his hands to pick up or clear the ball.

This rule means that it is worth chasing after the ball. You will rarely get to the ball first, but by putting pressure on the goalkeeper, you may force a mistake or a poor clearance which keeps your team on the attack.

The striker tries to force an error from the goalie.

The goalkeeper angles his clearance high and to the side, away from the approaching striker.

COMBINATION MARKING

A mixture of both man-to-man and zonal marking is often used at set plays. This is known as combination marking. The picture on the right shows combination marking being used to defend a long free kick. The defense is zonally marking, with one defender man-marking the opposition's dangerous striker, who may make a late run.

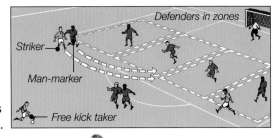

Defenders in zones

Striker

Man-marker

Free kick taker

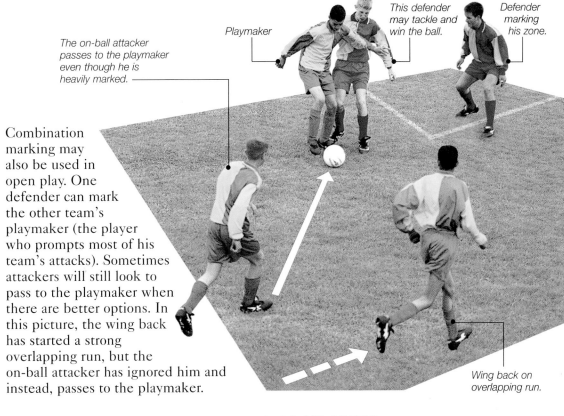

The on-ball attacker passes to the playmaker even though he is heavily marked.

Playmaker

This defender may tackle and win the ball.

Defender marking his zone.

Combination marking may also be used in open play. One defender can mark the other team's playmaker (the player who prompts most of his team's attacks). Sometimes attackers will still look to pass to the playmaker when there are better options. In this picture, the wing back has started a strong overlapping run, but the on-ball attacker has ignored him and instead, passes to the playmaker.

Wing back on overlapping run.

PENALTY SHOOT-OUTS

More and more games are being decided by penalty shoot-outs, with five penalties per side and 'sudden death' penalties if the scores are even. The coach chooses penalty-takers. Each coach has his own theory of the best order for his penalty-takers to play. Some prefer to save their best penalty-taker to last when the pressure is greatest. Others prefer to send him in first to put pressure on the other team. Whatever the order your team decides upon, if you are likely to be included, practice taking penalties often.

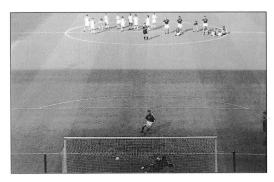

The Czech Republic score in a penalty shoot-out against France during Euro 96. See how the other players stand in the center circle as the penalties are taken.

COMMUNICATION

Communicating with your team on the field is essential. Many defensive mix-ups and breakdowns in attack are due to a lack of communication. Calls should be clear, and calm. Calling for the ball is a special skill. Only call when you're free. You can work on this by playing a five-a-side game where you can only receive a pass if you've called for it. If you don't call, but receive the ball, possession passes to the other side.

SOME COMMON CALLS AND SIGNALS

Sometimes, when there's a break in play, players get the chance to discuss situations and problems. Usually, though, calls are short and sharp as there is not time for anything else.

'Man-On!' – tells the on-ball player that an opposing player is approaching. Adding which side the player is coming from is even more helpful.

'Time' – tells a player about to receive or on the ball that he is unmarked and has space to turn and view the situation.

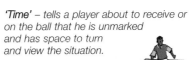

'Mine' – tells a teammate that you will take the ball.

Sometimes, teammates will warn you if you have the ball and are approaching the edge of the field.

Some signals are non-verbal. Here you can see a player signaling to his defense to push up quickly.

A team may have several free kicks which they have worked on in practice. This player is signaling to his teammates which kind of free kick he intends to take.

HEAD UP

Communication is not just about what you say or signal, it's also about being in a position to see what your teammates are doing and saying. For this, you need to have your head up and be aware of the game around you at all times. This is especially important when you are the player in control of the ball.

French international, Didier Deschamps has the ball at his feet, but is looking up to spot where his teammates are placed and what passes are possible.

FIVE V. TWO MINI GAME

This game helps communication skills. A team of two players act as defenders. They must try to get the ball from the team of five. The team with the ball are each numbered from one to five. One can only pass to two, two to three and so on. If player five manages to pass to player one, the team scores a point. Change the defenders once the side has scored three points.

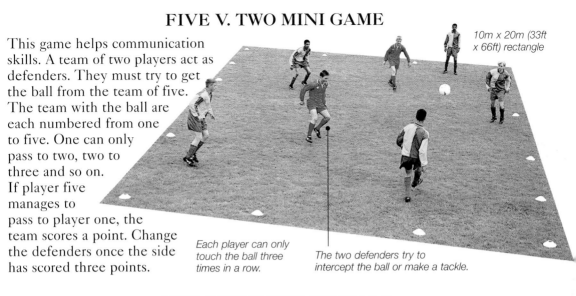

10m x 20m (33ft x 66ft) rectangle

Each player can only touch the ball three times in a row.

The two defenders try to intercept the ball or make a tackle.

THE REFEREE'S SIGNALS

The referee and his two assistants are in charge of the game. Don't argue with them. It doesn't help you or your team. Talking back may earn a yellow, or even a red card. Play until you hear the whistle.

Don't assume that a referee has seen a foul and stop playing. In the noise of a big game, it's not always possible to hear what the referee has said, so it's useful to know his signals.

Hand ball foul
Awarded for deliberate hand or arm contact.

Stand back ten yards
For the opposing team at a free kick.

Play on
The referee lets the play continue.

Indirect free kick
Given for obstruction.

Kicking foul
Player deliberately kicked.

Pushing foul
Player pushed off ball.

Foul throw-in
Feet over side-line.

Tripping foul
Player deliberately tripped.

PRE-GAME TACTICS

Be prepared for your game early. If possible, check out the field conditions beforehand. Make sure every player knows his role, especially new players or ones that have been off the team for some time. Your team's formations and tactics may have changed since a player previously played.

WARMING UP AND STRETCHING

Warming up before a game is a vital tactic. Stretching your muscles means you're less likely to get injured. Warming up exercises also help to make you more alert and ready for the game.

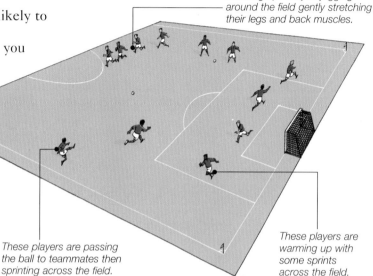

These players have just started warming up. They're jogging around the field gently stretching their legs and back muscles.

Pack long and short cleats and clothes to keep you warm and dry before and after the game. Goalkeepers should also take a towel to keep their gloves dry.

These players are passing the ball to teammates then sprinting across the field.

These players are warming up with some sprints across the field.

HAMSTRING STRETCH

Stand upright with one leg straight, a little in front of you. Slowly reach down. Don't bounce or move sharply. Hold for a count of ten, rise slowly and repeat.

GROIN STRETCH

Keep your feet pushed together.

Use your elbows to push your legs down gently.

Sit down with the soles of your feet pressing together and your hands on your knees. Press your knees down gently and hold this position for a count of ten.

CALF STRETCH

Extend your leg while keeping your other foot flat on the floor.

Bend one knee, stretching your other leg out behind you. Slowly push yourself down toward t̄⁻ ⁻⁻⁻⁻ and hold. Stan ⌐, and repeat with other leg.

CONCENTRATION

Concentration is important right from the moment just before the game starts. Watch how the opposing team lines up. Don't get caught by a quick break at the start.

From kick-off, this team attacks down the wing. The speed of the attack catches the defending team off guard.

Always think about your positioning. Be especially aware when the ball goes out of play or there's a free kick. You may be tempted to relax and rest, but the opposing team may choose just this time to strike.

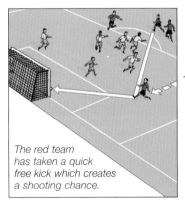

The red team has taken a quick free kick which creates a shooting chance.

Concentration wavers most when you're tired at the end of each half. Statistics show that this is also the time when goals are most likely to be scored. Make a special effort to concentrate at these times.

CONFIDENCE

Confidence is vital. If a player is nervous, he's more likely to make a mistake. Players lacking confidence are unlikely to carry out the team's tactics.

For example, a defender may be told to, 'attack when possible.' If the defender lacks confidence, he may decide that there is no opportunity to do so.

This attacker saw that the defender looked nervous so he decided to try and go past him.

This player is unconfident and believed he couldn't tackle the attacker. As a result he hasn't closed him down or made a challenge as quickly as he should have.

This player is chasing back to do his teammate's job. As a result he's let the attacker he was marking go free.

KEEPING CONFIDENCE

You can't win every game you play. Nor can you score in every game or be the player of the game every time. Even the best players make mistakes. The secret of success is not to get upset, but to practice hard and never stop trying your best on the field.

Before Euro 96, Alan Shearer hadn't scored in 12 England games. In Euro 96 he was top scorer.

INDEX

First published in 1997 by Usborne Publishing Ltd, 83-85 Saffron Hill, London EC1N 8RT, England.
Copyright © 1997 Usborne Publishing Ltd. AE. first published in America in March 1998.
The name Usborne and the device are Trade Marks of Usborne Publishing Ltd. All rights reserved.
No part of this publication may be reproduced, stored in a retrieval system or transmitted in any form or
by any means, electronic, mechanical, photocopying, recording or otherwise, without the prior
permission of the publisher.
Printed in Belgium.